Paul

God's Courageous Apostle

VOM BOOKS

Paul: God's Courageous Apostle

VOM Books
1815 SE Bison Rd.
Bartlesville, OK 74006

ISBN 978-0-88264-206-2

Written by The Voice of the Martyrs with Cheryl Odden

Illustrated by G. R. Erlan

Printed in the United States of America

For God's adventurers
—both young and old

A Note to Parents and Educators

The apostle Paul was the most prolific missionary in church history, traveling thousands of miles across the ancient Roman world to share the gospel. But Paul was not always a passionate follower of Christ. He was one of the early church's biggest enemies.

Paul, born as Saul, was a Pharisee from the tribe of Benjamin. He was named after Israel's first king, Saul. Tradition says that Paul's parents were prisoners of war who were enslaved by a Roman and taken to Tarsus. They were later freed and granted Roman citizenship.

Young Paul (then called Saul) went to Jerusalem to study under Rabbi Gamaliel, a member of the Sanhedrin. When the apostles were arrested and brought before the Sanhedrin, many of whom wanted to silence those who claimed Jesus as the Messiah, Gamaliel challenged the Sanhedrin: "Keep away from these men and let them alone; for if this plan or this work is of men, it will come to nothing; but if it is of God, you cannot overthrow it—lest you even be found to fight against God" (Acts 5:38,39). Paul did not heed his teacher's advice. He was present when Stephen was stoned to death, then hunted down and arrested Jesus' followers.

Paul's life as a Christ follower is told in sixteen chapters of the Book of Acts. He also wrote more than a dozen epistles in the New Testament. His writings are significant not only in teaching about the life, death, and resurrection of Jesus, but also in affirming that suffering for the sake of Christ is a normal part of Christian life and furthers the gospel message.

After his dramatic conversion on the road to Damascus, Paul went to Arabia where it is said he was taught by the Lord. Some believe God used this time to confirm the prophetic teachings of the Messiah. When he eventually returned to Jerusalem, believers viewed Paul with great caution. They could not believe this vicious persecutor of the church had become one of Christ's followers. From there, Paul traveled around sharing the message of Jesus as the Messiah and the free gift of salvation Christ offers to anyone who believes.

Paul is the biblical archetype of the suffering Christian. The Lord warned that he would suffer greatly for following Him (Acts 9:16), and he did. During Paul's three missionary journeys he was constantly harassed. His devotion to Christ put him in conflict with Jewish leaders, who could not accept that one of their own could believe Jesus was the Messiah. It infuriated them that he shared the gospel with Jews and especially with Gentiles (non-Jews).

The Jews' hatred toward Paul led to several attempts on his life. His presence stirred riots. Jews created such havoc around Paul that he was hauled to jail. His Roman citizenship proved especially valuable in his role as an evangelist. Invoking Roman citizenship allowed him audience with such influential figures as the Roman governor Felix, King Agrippa, and eventually the Roman emperor Nero. Roman citizenship probably saved his life more than once, but more important, it kept him on his missionary journey.

Nero even let Paul go free when he first appeared before him. Yet by the second time Paul appeared before Nero, Christ followers had become a scapegoat for Romans. Nero blamed Christians, Paul in particular, for the great Roman fire in AD 64. Historians say Nero also blamed Christians for spreading the "fire" of the gospel among Roman citizens. Early Christian tradition records that Paul was beheaded outside Rome, around the last year of Nero's reign, AD 69.

What is remarkable about the apostle Paul is his clear understanding of God's calling on his life. He skillfully used his Roman citizenship to promote the gospel, not preserve his life. His unyielding proclamation of the gospel was paramount to all things, even his own comfort, and outweighed his obedience to provincial authorities. Even as Paul exhorted everyone to "be subject to the governing authorities" (Romans 13:1), he makes clear in his actions in escaping from both Jewish and Roman authorities in Damascus that when it comes to spreading the gospel, the Kingdom comes first. Relentless in his evangelizing, Paul also knew when he had reached the end: "I have fought the good fight, I have finished the race, I have kept the faith" (2 Timothy 4:7).

While many books have focused on Paul's missionary journeys, this book tells the story of his sufferings for Christ. Though not comprehensive, the book shares the overcoming spirit of a man who persecutes Christ followers until he is brought face-to-face with Jesus for a greater purpose: to take the gospel to Jews and Gentiles. His heart is no longer filled with hate but with the love of Christ, for Christians and God's chosen people—the Jews. Though sharing the gospel brought him much suffering, it opened more doors for the gospel.

Children should understand that Jesus said following Him would lead to persecution (Luke 21:12; John 15:20). Persecution is a normal part of Christian life. It is not that we seek it out, but it happens when we obediently and graciously share the gospel with others. This is also a story of hope, challenging us to pray for those who oppose the gospel. May the story of Paul's sufferings for Christ inspire your children to call upon the power that He promises when we stand for Him, and may they run the race God has set out for them and run it well!

Saul patted the pouch on his hip as his horse galloped along the stone road.

He glanced back at the men riding with him to the city of Damascus.

Hmph! he thought smugly. *We'll finally get rid of those followers of Jesus for good!*

Saul and his men hunted down Christians all over Jerusalem, hauling them to prison. Like a wild man, Saul burst into homes dragging believers away. As word spread of the arrests, Jesus' followers fled to Damascus.

Saul looked at the pouch that held the papers to arrest the followers of Jesus in Damascus. *They won't be safe for long,* he thought. *No, they won't be safe for long.*

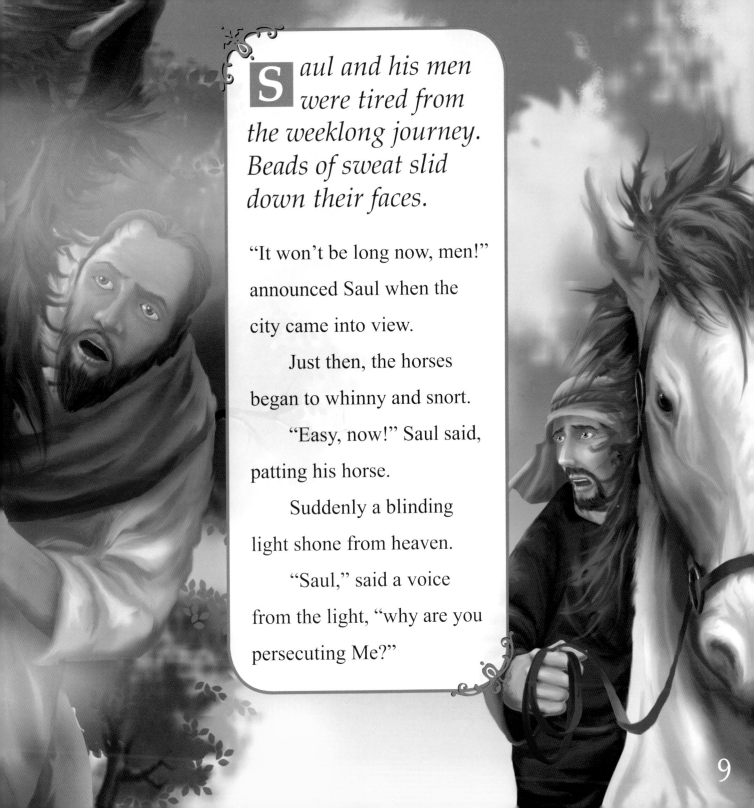

Saul and his men were tired from the weeklong journey. Beads of sweat slid down their faces.

"It won't be long now, men!" announced Saul when the city came into view.

Just then, the horses began to whinny and snort.

"Easy, now!" Saul said, patting his horse.

Suddenly a blinding light shone from heaven.

"Saul," said a voice from the light, "why are you persecuting Me?"

9

Saul fell to the ground. He squinted his eyes as he looked up into the light.

"Who—who are You, Lord?" Saul stammered.

Saul's men were surprised and confused. It wasn't like Saul to be at a loss for words.

"I am Jesus, the one you are persecuting."

What? thought Saul. He, too, was confused. *Is Jesus really God?*

"Get up and go to Damascus, where you will be told what to do."

The light and the voice disappeared. Saul stood up, but he was now blind.

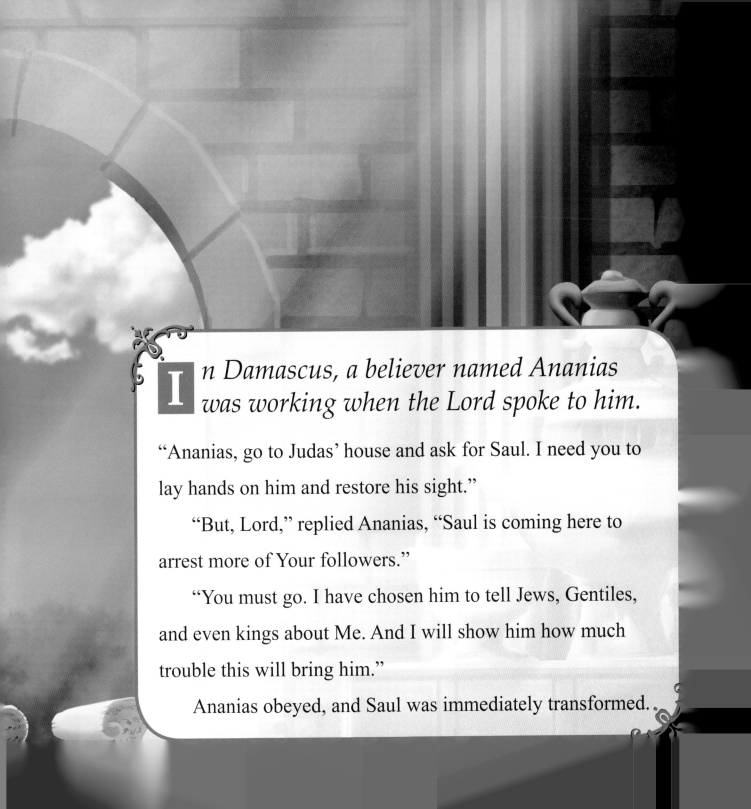

In Damascus, a believer named Ananias was working when the Lord spoke to him.

"Ananias, go to Judas' house and ask for Saul. I need you to lay hands on him and restore his sight."

"But, Lord," replied Ananias, "Saul is coming here to arrest more of Your followers."

"You must go. I have chosen him to tell Jews, Gentiles, and even kings about Me. And I will show him how much trouble this will bring him."

Ananias obeyed, and Saul was immediately transformed.

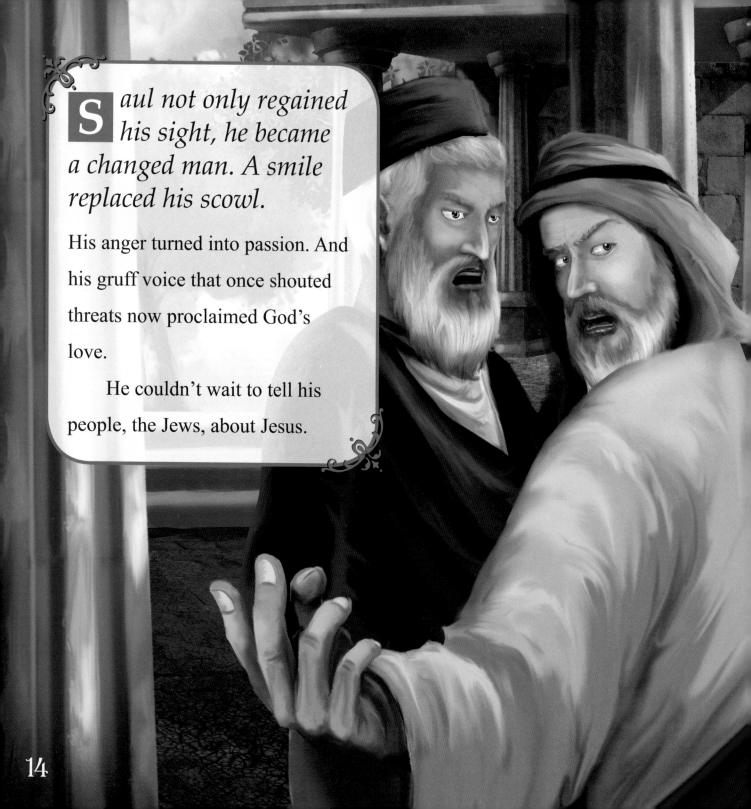

Saul not only regained his sight, he became a changed man. A smile replaced his scowl.

His anger turned into passion. And his gruff voice that once shouted threats now proclaimed God's love.

He couldn't wait to tell his people, the Jews, about Jesus.

"Isn't this the man who was arresting followers of Jesus?" Jews in Damascus murmured.

"Didn't he come to arrest more of them?" whispered others.

They were shocked that he believed Jesus was God's Son. They didn't like what Saul said, so they plotted to kill him.

16

When Saul heard of the Jews' plot to kill him, he knew it was time to leave. But Roman spies and the Jews were watching for him at the city gates.

Under the cover of night, believers placed Saul in a basket. They lowered him through a window and down the city wall until the basket reached the ground.

Saul was safe from trouble—for now.

When Saul returned to Jerusalem, he looked for Christ followers. "Why is he looking for us?" they asked.

A believer named Barnabas told them how Jesus had spoken to Saul and Saul believed Jesus was the Messiah. They gave thanks to God for changing the heart of this man who used to persecute them.

But Saul was restless. He needed to get the word out about Jesus. So he left Jerusalem, journeying by land and by sea, sharing with those he met. Soon, Saul became known as Paul. His name changed because his ministry had also changed. He now told the Gentiles, or those who are not Jews, about Jesus.

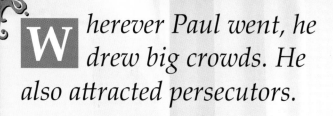

Wherever Paul went, he drew big crowds. He also attracted persecutors.

In Antioch, he preached in the synagogues where Jews worship. As he preached, his voice billowed through the synagogue doors and into the streets.

"Salvation through Jesus is for everyone!" he proclaimed. The following week, almost the entire city flocked to hear Paul.

"Who does he think he is, leading people away from our religion?" muttered Jewish leaders who were jealous of Paul. They left the synagogue with a plan to rid their town of this troublemaker.

21

As the jealous Jewish leaders stirred up trouble for Paul, those who heard his message told others.

Like feathers in the wind, the gospel spread far and wide. No one could stop it, not even angry religious and city leaders.

"Seize him!" cried one of the city leaders.

Suddenly the crowd turned on Paul. They pushed him through the city gate and forced him to leave. But that didn't stop Paul and his friends. He left for another city. The more the Jews and Gentiles pursued Paul, the more the gospel spread.

23

P aul preached to those who worshiped other gods. They, too, caused trouble for Paul. In Lystra, he healed a man who could not walk.

"You are a god!" shouted the people who witnessed the miracle. "We must worship you!"

"We are not gods!" Paul shouted over the roar of the crowd. "Turn to the living God!"

But the people wouldn't listen.

"Stone him!" yelled the group of Jews. These were the same Jews who had chased Paul out of other cities. The people pelted Paul with rocks. They dragged him outside the city and left him, thinking he was dead. But Paul was not dead. He got up, brushed off the dust, and went to a different city.

One night as Paul slept, he had a dream. "Come to Macedonia and help us!" a man in the dream begged Paul.

Paul awoke, packed up, and went there, preaching in a city called Philippi. Many placed their faith in Jesus. One was a slave girl who had made her owners rich by telling people about their futures. Now as a Christian, she would no longer be a fortuneteller. Her owners were angry. They grabbed Paul and took him to Roman authorities in the marketplace.

"This man is causing trouble," the slave owners said.

The Romans threw Paul in prison.

That night, Paul sat on the hard dirt floor, his feet chained to the wall. He did not cry or complain.

Instead, he and his friend Silas sang praises to God and prayed. As they did, the other prisoners listened.

Then the jail began to shake. The chains on the prisoners' feet broke loose from the wall and the cell doors burst open.

"We're free!" rejoiced a prisoner.

"Don't leave!" Paul said in his booming voice.

The prisoners obeyed.

29

Awakened by the earthquake, the prison keeper panicked when he saw the doors open.

"I'm going to get into so much trouble for letting the prisoners escape!" he said with a quiver. Then he heard a familiar voice.

"We're all still here!" cried Paul.

The prison keeper was so surprised that they hadn't run away. "What do I need to do to be saved?" the jailer asked. He wanted to follow Jesus, too.

The following morning, Paul and Silas were released from prison.

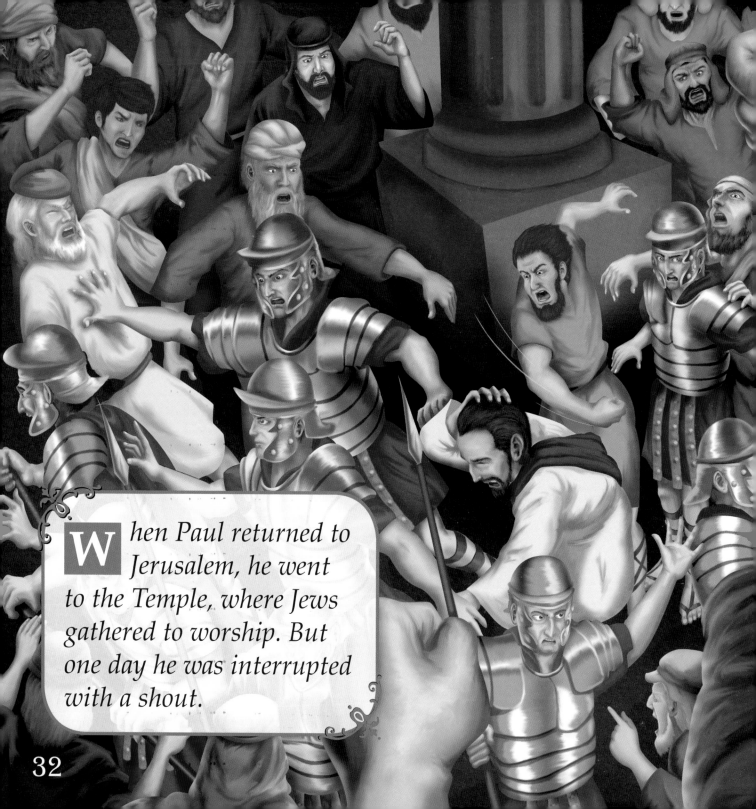

When Paul returned to Jerusalem, he went to the Temple, where Jews gathered to worship. But one day he was interrupted with a shout.

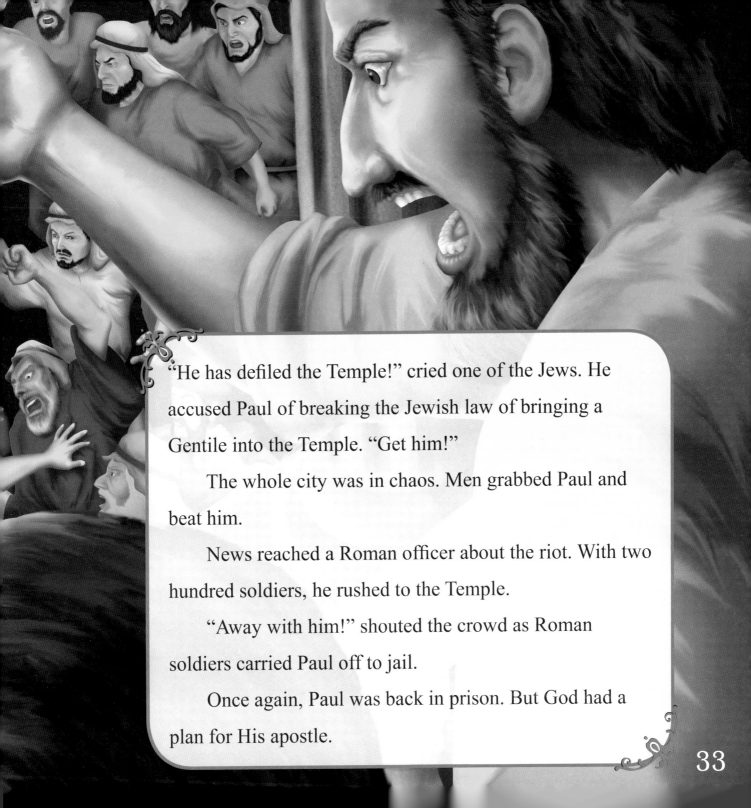

"He has defiled the Temple!" cried one of the Jews. He accused Paul of breaking the Jewish law of bringing a Gentile into the Temple. "Get him!"

The whole city was in chaos. Men grabbed Paul and beat him.

News reached a Roman officer about the riot. With two hundred soldiers, he rushed to the Temple.

"Away with him!" shouted the crowd as Roman soldiers carried Paul off to jail.

Once again, Paul was back in prison. But God had a plan for His apostle.

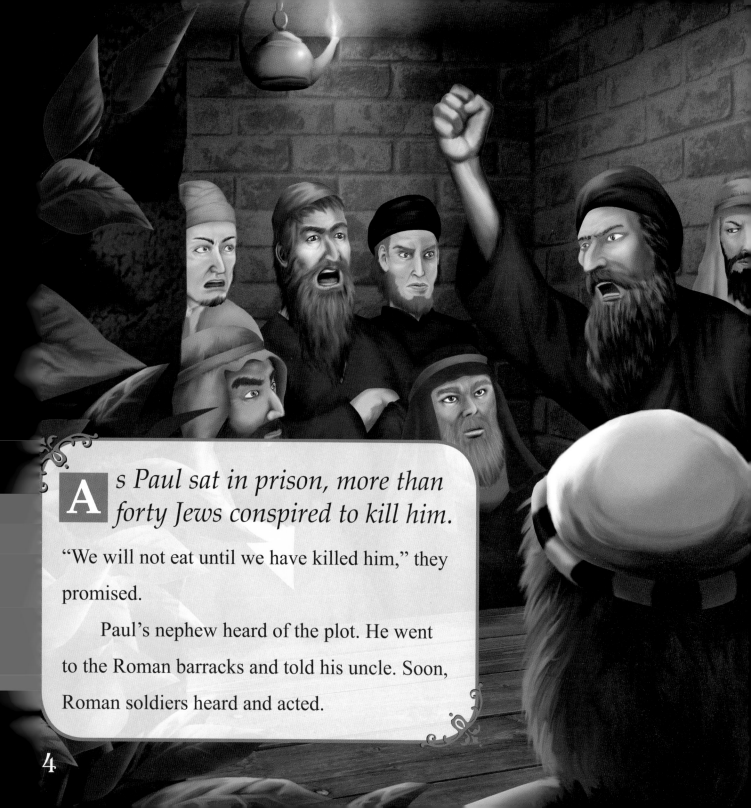

As Paul sat in prison, more than forty Jews conspired to kill him. "We will not eat until we have killed him," they promised.

Paul's nephew heard of the plot. He went to the Roman barracks and told his uncle. Soon, Roman soldiers heard and acted.

4

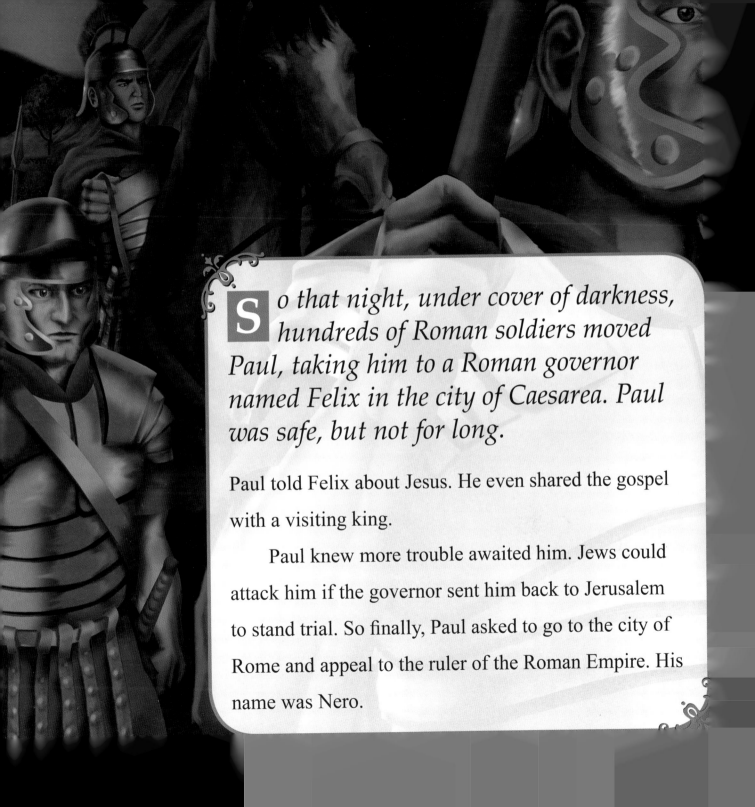

So that night, under cover of darkness, hundreds of Roman soldiers moved Paul, taking him to a Roman governor named Felix in the city of Caesarea. Paul was safe, but not for long.

Paul told Felix about Jesus. He even shared the gospel with a visiting king.

Paul knew more trouble awaited him. Jews could attack him if the governor sent him back to Jerusalem to stand trial. So finally, Paul asked to go to the city of Rome and appeal to the ruler of the Roman Empire. His name was Nero.

Paul boarded a ship for Rome. As he and the crew sailed, they faced a storm that lasted for days.

Everyone was afraid the ship would sink in the rough sea, even Paul. But one night, an angel of the Lord appeared to him.

"Don't worry, Paul," said the angel. "You are going to make it to Rome to appeal to Nero. You and the crew will all live."

Paul encouraged the crew with the angel's words. "Not one of you will lose a single hair from his head," he told them.

The ship was damaged. But, just as the angel had said, everyone landed safely on the shores of Malta.

39

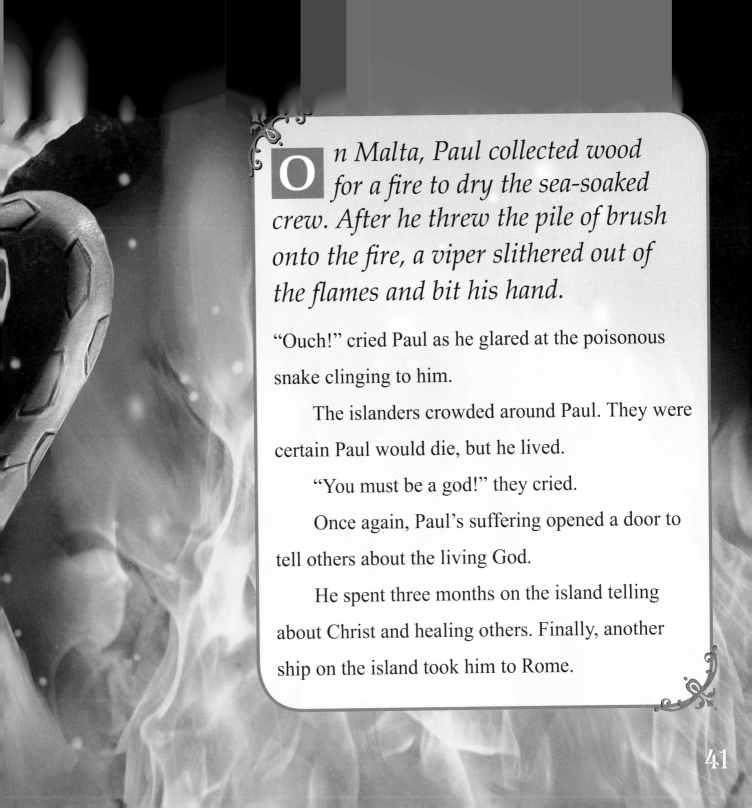

O n Malta, Paul collected wood for a fire to dry the sea-soaked crew. After he threw the pile of brush onto the fire, a viper slithered out of the flames and bit his hand.

"Ouch!" cried Paul as he glared at the poisonous snake clinging to him.

The islanders crowded around Paul. They were certain Paul would die, but he lived.

"You must be a god!" they cried.

Once again, Paul's suffering opened a door to tell others about the living God.

He spent three months on the island telling about Christ and healing others. Finally, another ship on the island took him to Rome.

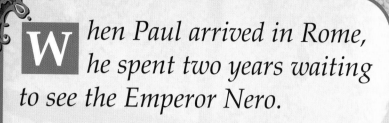

When Paul arrived in Rome, he spent two years waiting to see the Emperor Nero.

He didn't waste any time. He shared Christ with the Jews and anyone else who would listen. And as Paul told them about Jesus, the prison guards chained to Paul heard about him, too. Eventually Paul went before Nero. The emperor released him.

But Paul did not stop telling people about Jesus. Soon he was arrested again.

The Roman emperor Nero blamed Christians, including Paul, for setting the city of Rome on fire. Nero had Paul executed by beheading around AD 69.

43

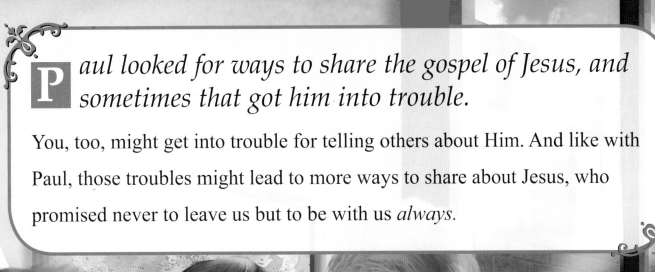

Paul looked for ways to share the gospel of Jesus, and sometimes that got him into trouble.

You, too, might get into trouble for telling others about Him. And like with Paul, those troubles might lead to more ways to share about Jesus, who promised never to leave us but to be with us *always*.

45

For Reflection

"But the Lord stood with me and strengthened me, so that the message might be preached fully through me, and that all the Gentiles might hear. Also I was delivered out of the mouth of the lion. And the Lord will deliver me from every evil work and preserve me for His heavenly kingdom. To Him be glory forever and ever. Amen!"
(2 Timothy 4:17,18)

When the Jews and others tried to arrest or kill Paul, how did that help him tell even more people about Jesus?

Have you ever gotten into trouble for telling someone about Jesus? If yes, what did you do? After reading Paul's story, what can you do?

Make a list of friends you would like to tell about Jesus. Ask Him to prepare their hearts, so they will listen to you and trust Jesus as their Savior and Lord.

Prayer

Dear Jesus,
Thank You for Paul's example of sharing the gospel even when it caused him a lot of trouble. Thank You for showing through Paul's life how these troubles can bring more opportunities to tell people about You. Help me have courage like Paul when I tell my friends about You. Help me praise You even if this causes trouble and they don't want to hear about You. Thank You that You are with us and will never leave us.

Amen.

Bibliography

Foxe, John and The Voice of the Martyrs. *Foxe: Voices of the Martyrs* (Bartlesville, OK: VOM Books, 2007).

Holman QuickSource Bible Atlas (Nashville, TN: Holman Bible Publishers, 2005).

Kent, Homer A., Jr. *Jerusalem to Rome: Studies in the Book of Acts* (Grand Rapids, MI: Baker Book House, 1972).

Van Braght, Thieleman J. *Martyrs Mirror* (Scottdale, PA: Herald Press, 1994).

Willmington, Dr. H. L. *Willmington's Guide to the Bible* (Wheaton, IL: Tyndale House Publishers, Inc., 1984).

The Voice of the Martyrs is a Christian nonprofit organization dedicated to helping those who are persecuted for their Christian witness in Communist, Islamic, and other nations hostile to Christ. In 1967, after being ransomed from Communist Romania, Richard and Sabina Wurmbrand came to the US and began their ministry to the persecuted church. Their vision was global, and a network of offices was birthed to raise awareness of, and take relief to, those suffering for their Christian witness.

For a free monthly newsletter and ways you can help today's persecuted church, contact:

The Voice of the Martyrs
1815 SE Bison Rd.
Bartlesville, OK 74006
(800) 747-0085
E-mail: thevoice@vom.org
Website: persecution.com
Youth website: kidsofcourage.com